MEDIUMSHIP

All You Need To Know

Richard Simonetti

First English Edition
© Copyright 2010 by
United States Spiritist Council
www.spiritist.us

First published in Portuguese in 2003 by CEAC Editora (www.ceac.
org.br), under the title Mediunidade, Tudo o Que Você Precisa
Saber.

English Version Translation: English Department of the Spiritist
Group Love and Light, New Jersey, U.S.A.

Translation Revision: Lorraine Arlotta, Robert Blakely, Ily Reis,
Jussara Korngold, Debi Caron and Livia Sasson.
Final Translation Revision: Mauricio Cisneiros

Electronic Version: Mauricio Cisneiros and Junara Araujo
Cover Design: Mauricio Cisneiros
Cover Image: Mozart Couto. Taken from the *Projeto Imagem* (The
Image Project) from the *Centro Espirita Francisco Xavier dos Santos*
(www.centroespiritafxs.com.br)

The English language version of this book is published and
distributed worldwide by the United States Spiritist Council.

Printed in the United States of America

Richard Simonetti is from Bauru, São Paulo, Brazil. He was born on October 10, 1935.

He comes from a Spiritist family and has participated in the Spiritist movement since very early in his life. He works at the Centro Espírita Amor e Caridade (Love and Charity Spiritist Center) (www.ceac.org.br), which offers substantial services in the areas of doctrinal teachings as well as social assistance and support.

Richard Simonetti was the first to voice the intention of developing a Spiritist Book Club, which is very instrumental in the dissemination of the doctrine in a number of cities. He is a prolific writer of articles for Spiritist newspapers and magazines, especially for Reformador [Reformer], Revista Internacional de Espiritismo [The International Spiritist Magazine], and Pagina Espirita [Spiritist Page].

He is retired from the Banco do Brasil (Bank of Brazil) and travels throughout Brazil and the world lecturing and disseminating Spiritism.

"Spirit phenomena have been contested by some individuals precisely because they appeared to be outside ordinary laws and because an explanation for them could not be found; however, provide them with a rational basis and there can be no more doubt. In this century, in which no one is satisfied with mere words, an explanation is therefore a powerful motive for conviction.

Thus, every day we see persons who have never even witnessed one phenomenon, who have never seen a table move or a medium write, but who are nevertheless as convinced as we are solely because they have read and understood. If we had to believe only what we have actually seen with our own eyes, our convictions would be reduced to insignificance."

Allan Kardec, *The Mediums' Book*, Part I, Chapter II, Item 17. (International Spiritist Council – First Edition - 2007)

TABLE OF CONTENTS

"Antipasto"

During the fraternal support services at the *Centro Espírita Amor e Caridade* (Love and Charity Spiritist Center) in Bauru, we often see people in truly disturbing situations:

-They see strange shadows;
-They hear things and don't know their origins;
-Objects appear and disappear mysteriously;
-Physical indispositions come and go without an exact diagnosis;
-Strange and shamelessly bold ideas in the mind;
-Contradictory feelings, alternating from euphoria to depression, from joy to sadness, from optimism to discouragement, occur mysteriously and inexplicably;
-Unjustifiable disagreements beset home life.

After we discard a great deal of imagination that is usually part of these reports, we consider the possibility that we're dealing with mediumistic phenomena which involve spirit interference.

These people become greatly distressed because they don't know the subject and think they're "sick in the head" or dealing with the devil.

Spiritism is a blessing that lights our path. It offers a broad view of the spirit world and provides knowledge of the mechanisms that govern contacts between those who live in the spirit realm and those who live here on Earth, who are still prisoners of the flesh.

***

The objective of these pages is to offer the reader an initiation into the domain of Spiritist knowledge, and to help people cope with physical phenomena of a spiritual origin. It's a basic necessity that we learn to control spirits so that they do not control us.

It's not our intention to write a treatise on the subject because, simply put, we're not competent enough. Moreover, the subject is perfectly explained in *The Mediums' Book,* which is indispensable reading to anyone interested in learning about the mechanisms that govern the interaction between the physical and spiritual planes.

This is only an introduction like antipasto for Italian people. I hope it proves tasteful to you so that you're motivated to go for the main course, the monumental book by Allan Kardec.

Enjoy and "buon appetito"!

Bauru, December 2002

Medium-person and Person-medium

1 – What is mediumship?
▶ In its simplest definition, mediumship is being sensitive to the influences of the spirit realm. It's the "sixth sense," which places us in contact with the world of the spirits; in much the same way as our senses of touch, taste, smell, seeing and hearing place us in contact with the world of humans.

2 – Does this mean that we are all mediums?
▶ All humans have the sensitivities that make the perception of spiritual influences possible. Not all humans, however, are sufficiently sensitive to produce mediumistic phenomena.

3 – What determines this difference?
▶ Let's imagine someone wearing a suit of armor that impairs their ability to hear and see what is happening around them. This is what happens with us when we reincarnate. We put on a dense flesh garment that inhibits our spiritual perceptions. A medium is someone who has an opening in this armor.

4 – Is it a physical type of opening? Is it in the body?
▶ Mediumship is a spiritual faculty inherent to all spirits. When we reincarnate it becomes dependent on the conditions of the body. In this regard, we can say that it's organic, because it's subordinate to a physical structure which doesn't inhibit all contact with the spirit world.

5 – Does it have anything to do with heredity?
▶ Mediumship is not subjected to genetics. The person who acts as an intermediary between the two planes is someone who was prepared for it in the spirit world; the person would have studied and undergone magnetic surgery in order to have the required sensitivity, in much the same way as the physical

body goes through an adaptive process.

6 – *When children of mediums experience mediumistic phenomena isn't there a genetic component to it?*
▶ In the same way that we have families of musicians and doctors we can have a family of mediums, not because of heredity but because of affinity. They're kindred spirits. They connect by blood ties to accomplish certain tasks.

7 – *Can we define mediumship as major or minor types?*
▶ We can define the medium-person condition inherent to human beings. All human beings feel the influence of spirits. And there are person-mediums; they're people who are endowed with a stronger sensitivity, which qualifies them for interaction with the beyond.

8 – *Wouldn't it be easier to use different terminology to distinguish one from the other, such as general and specific?*
▶ No, because these faculties aren't different in their essence; they're specialties only. For instance, there are people who have what is called a "musical ear." These people can reproduce any tune without studying. Then, there are people who are incapable of strumming the simplest song. In both cases, it's a characteristic of the same faculty - hearing. Something similar happens with mediumship. We all have "ears" to hear the spirit world. Some people "hear" better than others and this gives them the ability to communicate with spirits.

Spirit Influence

1 – *Generally speaking, people have difficulty in keeping emotional stability. They go from sadness to joy, from*

14

depression to euphoria, from a good mood to a bad one. These emotions aren't always associated with what happens daily in our lives. Does this have anything to do with mediumship?

▶ No doubt! Cyclothymiacs[1], an unexplainable diversity of emotional states, is associated with the nature of the spirits that come closer to us and is responsible for the influence under which we suffer.

2 – Are you referring to the souls of the dead?

▶ Yes, they're discarnate beings free from matter but shackled to human interests. They stay around us and influence us. They motivate us and even guide us. In question 459 of *The Spirits' Book*, spirit mentors who answered Kardec's questions confirmed that this influence is so intense that it's often greater than we suppose and we confuse their thoughts with our own.

3- Why do they do that? What's their purpose?

▶ Their motives depend on their level of development. There are those who are confused and want help, those who amuse themselves by annoying us, those who want revenge, have addictions and need intermediaries to satisfy themselves.

4 – How can we distinguish our thoughts from those inspired by a discarnate being?

▶ It's difficult at first because the mental flow of the spirits with whom we associate is expressed in our minds as our own thoughts, or as something coming from within ourselves.

5 – Does this mean that our thoughts, as well as our emotions,

---

1   Translator's Note: Cyclothymia - an emotional condition characterized by alternate periods of elation and depression. In its more severe form called *manic-depressive psychosis*.

are simply reflections of what is going on with the spirits near us?

▶ Exactly. We also need to consider attunement factors. Usually, these entities are compatible with the way we are; with our tendencies and our ideas.

6 – According to this principle, is it possible, for example, for a spirit to make a person commit suicide even if that person would never think of such a thing?

▶ Yes, if the discarnate being is able to instill in the person a desire to kill him or herself, but, certainly, this person has to like the idea, accept it and even nurse it.

7 – How can we overcome these negative influences and make ourselves able to receive only positive ones?

▶ In question number 469 of *The Spirits' Book*, Kardec asked the same question. The mentor stated categorically, "Do only what is right and put all your trust in God." This is a valuable program to free ourselves from negative influences.

8 – How does this work?

▶ Our trust in God sustains emotional equilibrium in difficult situations, thus avoiding depressive states of mind, which make us vulnerable to lower influences. Doing what is right synchronizes us with the sources of life and gives us the infallible protection of spirit benefactors.

Spiritual Maladjustment

1 – Often, a person who has problems that include depression, anxiety and chronic illnesses, hears from people at a Spiritist Center: "You're a medium." Should that person develop their mediumship in order to be cured?

▶ This is the advice from less informed Spiritist directors. We cannot confuse spiritual maladjustments with the development of mediumship.

2 – But there are cases when a person experiences phenomena like seeing and perceiving spirits...
▶ If the person is tense, sick and nervous because of existential problems, he or she will experience a psychic super-excitation that may cause them to see and perceive the spirit world. It doesn't mean that they're mediums and need development.

3 – What should be done in this case?
▶ Submit to spiritual treatment at a well-directed Spiritist Center where there is a fraternal support program. The person can also talk to a friend who is knowledgeable about the process to restore physical and psychic stability.

4 – When you say a well-directed Spiritist Center, do you mean that there are centers that don't have good directors?
▶ Unfortunately, yes. There are cases in which directors aren't concerned with Spiritism's basic books, particularly *The Mediums' Book,* which is used to study mediumship. They practice a 'home-grown' type of Spiritism, far from the customary.

5 – How can a person know if his or her problems are due to budding mediumship or mere consequences of spiritual maladjustment?
▶ At first, the person should not worry about this. Even if the person is a medium in need of development, it's fundamental that he or she undergo the spiritual treatment first and correct the maladjustment. Later, they can look into the possibility of being a medium.

6 – *But if the person is a medium how can he or she correct the maladjustment if they don't attend mediumistic classes?*
► A person's equilibrium isn't dependent on participating in mediumistic work. The person's presence in such a meeting is counter-productive. If the person is a medium, his or her abilities will be amplified and they won't know how to control them. The maladjustment will be aggravated.

7 – *What does this spiritual treatment consist of?*
► Basically, regular magnetic passes, writing the person's name in a prayer book at a meeting which is appropriate for this purpose, use of magnetized water, assimilation of doctrinal teachings at public meetings and reading the suggested Spiritist books.

8 – *Often a person is under medical care. In this case, what happens?*
► The person must be told that spiritual treatment doesn't preclude medical treatment. They must be told that psychic abilities are exacerbated by spirit influences and that mediumistic maladjustments have repercussions in the physical body. Often, the problem requires medical attention. The ideal, then, is to have both treatments.

Environmental Influences

1 – *It isn't easy to find a person who has perfect emotional and physical stability. Does this have anything to do with mediumistic sensitivity?*
► It has everything to do with it. We're immersed in an ocean of mental waves that are emitted by incarnate and discarnate spirits. We can be contaminated by viruses and bacteria. We can also suffer from spiritual contamination which changes

our state of mind.

2 – *Does this explain why a person tends to feel depressed at funerals and happy at weddings?*
▶ No doubt. The situation and environment exert a great influence. I remember the death of Ayrton Senna[2]. It caused a tremendous reaction in the public, even those who did not follow his feats in the racing circuit. Emotions expand and can draw masses in.

3 – *Does this also explain atrocities committed by soldiers during war?*
▶ Wars produce appalling epidemics of cruelty because of our inferiority. Cruelty has free access to hearts that are still controlled by animalistic instincts. It spreads like wild fire.

4 – *It sounds like what happens in homes. People loose control and attack each other; they scream and curse and often resort to physical aggression.*
▶ There is not a better place for this inferiority to be demonstrated. Social customs are forgotten in the home. People show who they really are. The environment is disturbed because we are not saints on earth. It becomes an ideal place for aggressive behavior to spread; all family members are involved.

5 – *How can we avoid this?*
▶ It's necessary to strengthen and develop spiritual defenses by raising our vibratory levels and tuning into frequencies that place us above the disturbances in the environment.

---

2 Translator's Note: **Ayrton Senna da Silva**, (March 21, 1960 – May 1, 1994) was a Brazilian racing driver and three time Formula One world champion. He was killed while leading the 1994 San Marino Grand Prix.

6 – How does this attunement process work?

▶ Let's consider radio transmissions. They expand in specific frequencies. In order to listen to a particular station we turn the dial and tune in to that frequency. Our minds are powerful emitters and receptors of vibrations, so we tend to tune in to frequencies that are similar to ours.

7 – What should we do to connect with a healthy frequency?

▶ In principle, we should consider that it's determined by the nature of our thoughts. There is an old saying that goes: *"Tell me who your friends are and I'll tell you who you are."* We can also say: *"Tell me the nature of your thoughts and I'll tell you what influences you assimilate."*

8 – Does this mean that balance or unbalance, peace or chaos, joy or sadness, aggression or gentleness depend essentially on us?

▶ Exactly. Although our psychic and physical problems can be amplified by the environment, their origins are in our thoughts and behaviors. It's vital that we think and do good if we want good to be present in our lives.

Magnetic Passes

1 – What is a magnetic pass when it's administered at a Spiritist Center?

▶ In its simplest expression, a magnetic pass is a donation of magnetic energy; much like a blood transfusion. For instance, if the patient has anemia a blood transfusion revitalizes the patient's blood. Likewise, if the person has problems associated with the soul, expressed as anxiety and disturbances, a pass helps the recovering process.

2 – *How do you define this magnetism?*
▶ Magnetism is a form of energy that living beings release by an act of their will. It's controlled and emitted during a pass. That is what pass-givers do when they stand by patients with intent to assist.

3 – *Is the pass-giver a medium?*
▶ Not in the literal sense. The pass-giver is not in a trance or serving as a channel. However, the person has the indispensable cooperation from spirit benefactors who control the service. They emit spiritual magnetism which makes the pass more efficient because it's complemented by human magnetism.

4 – *Is a pass only useful for problems of the soul?*
▶ It helps all our problems, physical as well as psychic. When a person is unable to cope with certain life situations they suffer from what we call 'magnetic hemorrhage'. The person loses strength and becomes fragile, thus they become vulnerable to harmful spirit influences. A pass helps by revitalizing the person and stopping the hemorrhage.

5 – *What is the basic requirement for a person to be benefited by a pass?*
▶ Faith. This is very clear in Jesus' teachings. He used to explain the benefits of his healings by saying: "*Your faith has healed you.*" The Master did not grant faith. He only demonstrated that without faith it's difficult to establish attunement with the pass-giver.

6 – *What should be the person's attitude at the time of a pass?*
▶ The person should be praying sincerely and asking for Divine protection. There is another important factor beyond prayer and faith: merit. As Jesus taught: *to each according to his merit.* The feelings we have at that time are important, but

21

it's also fundamental that we practice the good always.

7 – A pass stops 'magnetic hemorrhaging'?
▶ When a patient suffers from anemia because of internal hemorrhaging, a blood transfusion is just palliative. It's necessary to treat the problem with medicine or surgery. Something similar occurs with weakening magnetism; the causes must be resolved or the treatment won't have a lasting effect.

8 – How can we manage this, considering our daily problems and annoyances?
▶ Sickness doesn't happen because of difficulties that are typical of human existence. The problem is in the way we cope. If we cultivate understanding, tolerance, patience, compassion and the other virtues taught and exemplified by Jesus, we'll avoid the verbal and mental outbursts which facilitate the maladjustments that disturb us.

Pass Givers

1 – Is there a special characteristic that qualifies someone to give passes?
▶ The emission of magnetic energy depends on a person's will; therefore we all do it unconsciously at different times independent of special conditions.

2 – Daily?
▶ Exactly. A mother comforting a child, a doctor treating a patient, a teacher while teaching, or a person caring for a plant, all are identified by a common thread: they emanate magnetism that enfolds the beneficiary.

22

3 – *And what are the results?*

▶ If done with dedication and pass-givers love what they are doing, they can obtain prodigious results: the child calms down, the patient improves, students behave better, and the plant thrives.

4 – *In order to administer a pass at a Spiritist Center is the desire to serve and good will enough?*

▶ They're important factors but because it's a specialized activity the person must take a course and accept the discipline contained therein.

5 – *Do Spiritist Centers teach this course?*

▶ They must! One of the requirements for a well-directed center is that skilled monitors be put in charge of preparing people who want to join the pass-giver's team.

6 – *Are there several techniques to administering a pass?*

▶ Yes, however they require further specialized studies. During public meetings at Spiritist Centers, the imposition of the hand is sufficient, provided there is intent to help with good energy.

7 – *Basically, what are the disciplines for this service?*

▶ Besides doctrinal knowledge related to magnetism, a pass-giver must live a healthy life in two aspects: Physical – no vices, good diet, exercise, good personal hygiene, disciplined work; Spiritual – cultivate Evangelical virtues, study, meditation, prayer.

8 – *Can a pass-giver who isn't prepared to serve or one that has vices or mental confusion, harm people while giving a pass?*

▶ It would be possible if a pass-giver wished to use negative energy to do harm to others. But, in normal circumstances,

23

pass-givers have good intentions or the will to help others. If the pass-giver isn't in a good condition, but their intent is to heal, the pass they administer becomes null. They must have the potential intensity and purity which makes this service efficient.

Exoticism

1 – There have been cases in which people take their relatives' clothes to certain Spiritist Centers to be magnetized. Does it work?

▶ The result is not satisfactory because clothes are not good receptors for magnetism. And consider that the fluids deposited in them are unstable and depend on attunement, which includes the beneficiaries' faith. It's a bit complicated. Usually, the person doesn't even know that it is being done.

2 – In the same line of thought, can we apply this logic to defense baths and smoke outs which are recommended to avoid impure spirits?

▶ Defense baths, which use herbs and salts, have medicinal properties. They may bring a measure of well-being. Smoke outs perfume the place and keep mosquitoes out.

3 – Don't they have any spiritual effect?

▶ It's risky and depends on the nature of the tormenting entities. If they have sharp intelligences and are conscious of what they are doing they think it's all very amusing. Smoke outs have no influence on them. On the other hand, there's a question of faith. If the person believes that these practices have a positive spiritual effect, then the person reacts favorably and feels strengthened; thus inhibiting the effects from obsessors.

24

4 – *And exorcism by orthodox churches? They seem to work in some cases.*

► If it's a disturbed and unfortunate spirit, a needy one who isn't aware of what is going on we may be able to remove it with ritualistic practices by scaring it away. If the spirit is aware of what it's doing then it just laughs.

5 – *How about amulets, horseshoes, chains, rabbit's foot, stones, images...*

► They can neutralize harmful influences, if the person really believes in them, not because of an amulet's value but because of the persons' faith. When someone is certain that they're protected, they mobilize their own defenses.

6 – *From Spiritism's point of view is any of this advisable?*

► A Spiritist person is called upon to change this type of mindset. We must be liberated from external practices, rituals, and chants and everything else that involves conditioning and dependency.

7 – *How can we deal with existential problems and negative spirit influences without these practices?*

► Our spiritual defenses must be based on constant study, constructive meditation, solidarity, and work on inner transformation, genuine praying habits, and discipline of our feelings. These are the things that improve our vibrations and protect us from any negative influences.

8 – *Why isn't this orientation followed by all Spiritist Centers?*

► It's because when they try to tend to human health problems they serve as hospitals for psychic and physical ailments. They neglect doctrinal teachings which are more important. A Spiritist Center must be, above all, a school where we learn to cope with life's challenges in a balanced and productive way. We should value the school so that we don't need the hospital.

Initiation

1 – *Aside the resources that a Spiritist Center mobilizes in favor of people with physical and spiritual problems, what else can be done?*
▶ The most important part is up to the interested person. They're responsible for following the orientation they receive. We reiterate that learning Spiritism is fundamental. It's where we find the program for our spiritual growth and the ability to overcome the obstacles that afflict us.

2 – *How does this learning happen?*
▶ It happens with attendance to doctrinal meetings, Spiritist courses which every well-directed center must offer and, above all, reading and studying Spiritist books. Books are, without a doubt, the most efficient resource during this learning process. They're always available. They can go with us everywhere and are ready to impart knowledge anytime; they repeat the lesson until we assimilate it.

3 – *Which books would you recommend to a beginner?*
▶ It's necessary to consider a person's culture and familiarity with Spiritist Literature. If the person is a reader, accustomed to focusing their attention on something, he or she must read first *The Spirits' Book, The Mediums' Book,* and *The Gospel According to Spiritism.* In these three books by Kardec, we have the triple aspect of the doctrine in order: philosophy, science, and religion.

4 – *Why only this type of reader? They're a minority in our country!*

► These basic books were written in Paris during the 19th century. At the time, Paris, the City of Light, was the most cultured in the world. The language used is difficult to understand for those who aren't used to reading, which is the case for the majority of the Brazilian population.

5 – The Gospel According to Spiritism is the best selling Spiritist book. Isn't this proof that it's assimilated well?
► Yes. No doubt the book sells well but, unfortunately, it's not read that much. Rarely, it's truly appreciated by people who frequent Spiritist Centers. For many Spiritist directors the book has magical properties. They recommend: *"At any difficult time, open it at random and read it. The spirits will cause the book to open on the appropriate passage. As you read all bad influences are removed."*
There are people who suggest that, depending on the person's need, the spirits make people see text that isn't in the book. It's pure magic and it's incompatible with the reasoning that Kardec professed.

6 – Should we substitute the codification[3] with other books when we recommend reading for beginners?
► The codification is always the first choice. It's Spiritism's base and foundation. We should avoid recommending it only if the person cannot
possibly understand it. We can then start with an easier book.

7 – Are there beginner's books in your bibliography?
► There are several, among them "Uma Razão Para Viver"[4]

---

3   Translator's Note: Codification refers to the five books compiled by Allan Kardec: The Spirits' Book, The Mediums' Book, The Gospel According to Spiritism, Heaven and Hell and Genesis.
4   Translator's Note: A great choice for beginners is the book "*Spiritist Philosophy*" by the Allan Kardec Educational Society.

[A Reason to Live] which is similar to a spelling book for people who need orientation and help. It works as a small Spiritist course. It covers Spiritism's basic topics and includes instructions to the reader at the end of every chapter.

8 – *What other books would you recommend?*
► The Spiritist bibliography is extensive. I reiterate that Allan Kardec's books are the best initiation. However, the person who recommends them must have a good sense of whether the reader is be able to appreciate them or they'll be relegated to serving as library ornaments.

Mediumistic Initiation

1 – *Are there mediumistic courses at Spiritist Centers?*
► Some are organized to offer them and provide disciplined and efficient programs in this area. It's a service that must be instituted at every Spiritist Center as their directors become aware of their importance.

2 – *What's the advantage for a person who is not a medium?*
► I reiterate that we are all in constant contact with the spirit world. Knowledge about the mechanism that controls this connection is fundamental
for our stability. The great majority of physical and psychic problems that afflict us are directly related to actions from disturbed or disturbing spirits.

3 – *Isn't the help we get when we attend doctrinal meetings and receive passes at a Spiritist Center enough?*
► When somebody has a wound it's not enough to shoo the mosquitoes

away. We must heal it. The resources available at a Spiritist Center can take tormenting spirits away but they may return or others may come.

4 – *Do we need to close the door?*
▶ Exactly. Jesus made a momentous pronouncement about this. He said that one unclean spirit who is removed returns with others and the victim's situation gets worse. Consequently, we need to develop our own defenses. This implies a change in attitude toward life and requires the discipline to study and learn.

5 – *How do they work and how long do these courses last?*
▶ There are no rigid rules. It depends on the availability of the center and instructors' preparation. A course of two years is reasonable. The first year covers basic topics in Spiritism and the second year covers mediumship.

6 – *What can a person do if the center doesn't offer courses in Spiritism and mediumship?*
▶ If the person is well adjusted in a center they shouldn't stop going there; they should look for a place where they can take these courses. Centers don't always value these courses and this is a mistake. The best way to learn is in a classroom environment with monitors, curriculum, regular classes, including attendance and study commitments.

7 – *There are people who complain that when they start studying Spiritism, more problems appear in their lives, especially on days that they have classes. Why does this happen?*
▶ It's natural. These are the "mosquitoes" that try to stop the wound from healing. They're "friends" who want to stop us from developing defense mechanisms that can neutralize their influence. They try to discourage us by creating problems.

8 – *Don't our spirit mentors protect us?*

► They're not baby sitters at our beck and call. Their function is to guide, usually by using intuition to show us better ways. They cannot walk for us or carry us. We need to maintain attendance and interest in learning. If we persist, our "friends" leave and stop bothering us.

Reasons to Participate

1 – *Must every Spiritist participate in mediumistic meetings?*

► Certainly, it's the transcendental part of Spiritism. It was through them that Allan Kardec developed the codification. The name "Doctrine of the Spirits" suggests an interaction with the beyond to help us sustain our ideals.

2 – *There are people who say that the time for phenomena has past and that we should be concerned with the dissemination of Spiritist principles and their application in society.*

► It's a mistaken and dangerous notion. Negligence of the interaction that Jesus and the primitive community maintained with the spirit world was one of the factors that precipitated Christianity's deviation from its original path.

3 – *What if the person doesn't have mediumship to be developed?*

► A mediumistic meeting isn't made up of mediums only. There are directors, people who help with counseling, pass-givers, and most importantly, supporting members who provide psychic support with their attention and good will.

4 – *Besides cultivating the transcendental part of Spiritism, is there any other benefit?*

► Yes, starting with the spiritual assistance we receive. At this time, spirit benefactors can help more effectively, with magnetic applications, guidance and removal of entities that may be disturbing us, commonly called "attachments."

5 – Anything else?
▶ It's a blessed opportunity to follow one of Spiritism's basic tenets – to practice charity. There are crowds of tormented spirits who aren't aware of their condition but are ready to be helped. The meeting is a light for their journey; for participants it's illumination for their hearts.

6 – Is there any other repercussion in our lives?
▶ No doubt! It serves as a mirror showing us what our future can be if we don't cultivate values of Goodness and Truth. It's as though they're warning us: *"Be careful! We are what you can be tomorrow if you do not pay attention!"*

7 – What if the person doesn't like mediumistic meetings?
▶ We cannot always do what we like! For our own good, we must learn to like the things we need to do, especially when we're called to participate in productive and edifying activities such as the interaction with the beyond.

8 – What should we do to help this state of mind?
▶ Knowledge is fundamental. When we study Spiritism, especially the principles of mediumistic work, we become aware of the benefits that we'll be providing and reaping. We then find goodwill which is the basis for a pleasant, efficient activity. That is why it's important to have mediumistic courses to explain the subject to people.

Suffering Spirits

1 – What does the expression "suffering spirit" mean?
▶ A suffering spirit is someone who is attached to impressions and anguishes of physical life. They feel perplexed, afflicted and usually wander aimlessly, unaware of their condition.

2 – What's the usefulness of letting them manifest?
▶ These spirits wander around like somnambulists and aren't aware of the spiritual reality. When they come in contact with the energies in the room and the medium's energy, they feel revitalized and awakened enough to talk to an indoctrinator[5].

3 – Why an "indoctrinator"?
▶ Actually, this term is inadequate because when a spirit is in such state of mental disorder it's incapable to understand doctrinal information. But, the term has been established because of general use. The indoctrinator/counselor is the person who talks to them. It could be the meeting's director or another team member after appropriate training.

4 – What does an indoctrinator/counselor do?
▶ The main objective is to help the spirit with the trauma experienced during the so called "passage." If the cause of death was an accident, for instance, the impressions and the agony of the moment continue in the form of endless torment. The counselor should speak firmly, but with gentle determination. They explain that the spirit is no longer living that incident, that they're in an emergency room, that they received medical treatment and have started rehabilitation.

---

5   Translator's Note: 'Counselor' is more appropriate in this case and generally used nowadays.

5 – *And will the spirit be informed that he has died?*

▶ This is a mistake many counselors make. They even direct the spirit: *"Go up brother! You no longer belong in the living world."* Go where? Wrong expression! The spiritual plane is a projection of the physical one. It's another dimension and it interpenetrates ours. To tell him that he died may worsen his condition. The shock is too great.

6 – *When is the spirit informed?*

▶ In the book *And Life Goes On* channeled by Francisco Candido Xavier[6], Andre Luiz explains that we must allow the spirit to realize its condition. He describes a hospital where patients lived for months without knowing that they had passed away. This does not mean that they should never be told. It means it should be an exception, when we feel that the spirit is "mature" enough to face spiritual life.

7 – *Wouldn't this assistance be done more efficiently by spirit mentors?*

▶ Yes, if the conditions were favorable. During the period of adjustment to spirit life, the spirit is traumatized and incapable of noticing the presence of spirit mentors. Hence, there is a need to manifest at a Spiritist Center.

8 – *Considering the number of people who die on a daily basis, mediumistic groups probably don't help even one percent of them. What happens to the rest?*

▶ When a person is burned and there are no specialized

---

6   Francisco Cândido Xavier, affectionately known as Chico; (April 2, 1910 – June 30, 2002) was a celebrated medium in Brazil´s Spiritist movement. In his life he wrote more than 400 books by a process known as automatic or channel writing.

medical facilities nearby, an ill-equipped doctor will treat the person in his own office. It's the same with spirits that are alienated from spiritual reality. Spirit mentors don't abandon them because there are no specialized mediumistic groups available. They work without the needed human magnetism. This is why a well-structured group operates as a progressive emergency room. They serve a minority today. They will serve multitudes tomorrow as their services are expanded.

Private Meetings

1 – Why don't some Spiritist Centers hold public mediumistic meetings?
► It would be more correct to ask why some do. Mediumistic meetings should be private due to their nature and because they require a harmonious environment.

2 – What is a harmonious environment?
► It's an environment where all participants agree on the meeting's objectives and wish to establish a communion with the spirits. This requires a familiarity with the subject, and that cannot be expected of sporadic participants. These eventual participants attend the meetings without knowledge about spirit interaction.

3 – What happens when the environment isn't harmonious?
► The mediums have difficulty in connecting with the communicating spirit's thoughts and the spirit finds difficulty in expressing them. The potential benefit for the suffering entity is then jeopardized. And there is another problem: people suffering from spiritual maladjustments may produce animistic manifestations (their own souls manifest), or unbalanced spirits may disrupt the meeting.

4 – *Couldn't people be made aware of the seriousness of the subject?*

▶ A public meeting entails multitudes of people which in itself is an obstacle to harmony. The other problem is a heterogeneous environment. Neophytes without any knowledge about spirit interactions think that manifestations are strange phenomena anyway. Usually, they think all of it's ridiculous therefore there's a tendency to disturb instead of help.

5 – *What should we think of Spiritist Centers who have public mediumistic meetings and claim that they're efficient and help many people?*

▶ This may happen occasionally. At any rate, we should consider two Spiritist principles: First, we need to follow Allan Kardec's orientation in *The Mediums' Book.* He makes it very clear that a person needs to prepare for a mediumistic meeting by becoming familiar with the phenomenon, and this takes time and commitment to study. Secondly, we need to make an effort to optimize the meeting.

6 – *What does optimize mean?*

▶ As the word suggests, it means to make it optimal, make it reach its goals completely. A public mediumistic meeting may benefit persons but only potentially; let's say only about forty percent of the time. To optimize it means to raise it to one hundred percent. This can only be done if it's private and the number of participants is decreased. It means to have conscientious and knowledgeable people who are attuned to the objectives of the exchange.

7 – *Spiritist Centers that hold public mediumistic meetings claim that if they restrict them they lose attendees because people want contact with spirits.*

▶ If the center has fraternal service with interviews, passes, energy work[7], a recommended reading list, Spiritism and mediumship study groups, attendance tends to increase, not decrease. Experience has proven this.

8 – *There are mediums with good potentials that are used to this practice. If we consider their merits wouldn't it be problematic to impose changes?*
▶ No doubt, we need to be careful. But, it's possible to minimize the problem with refreshing courses and seminars, that's when discipline can be emphasized. It's easier to accept new things when they are explained and there is preparation. In summary: let's change people's minds before we change the work they do.

Direction of the Work

1 – *There are times when, if the director is absent, the meeting is cancelled. How can this problem be resolved?*
▶ Mediumistic meetings cannot be affected by continuity problems. It's inconceivable that any mediumistic activity is suspended because of a coordinator's absence.

2 – *What if the director claims that there is no one fit to substitute?*
▶ A certificate of incompetence is given to this person. One of the director's functions is to train group members to fill in at any eventual absence. It's their job to prepare others to direct the meeting and the counseling dialogue with the spirits.

---

7   Translator's Note: Energy work will be discussed in subsequent chapters of this book.

3 – *More than one?*
► At least two or three, so that the likelihood of postponing the meeting is as remote as possible; postponements frustrate the spirit mentors with regard to the activities they programmed.

4 – *Wouldn't it be better to have a course for directors of mediumistic meetings?*
► No doubt! Let's consider, however, that the best way to learn to direct a meeting is to do it, as much as the best way to learn to talk to spirits is to talk to them. The practical aspect is more important than the theoretical.

5 – *Do you train Spiritist directors?*
► I usually select three or four people from the teams that I monitor for this purpose. I rotate the training program, starting with counseling.

6 – *Beyond practice and study, what makes a good counselor?*
► Empathy. The ability to feel the spirit's problems, as well as the ability to get the spirit's attention and help with whatever difficulty the spirit has. And it's also essential to enjoy this type of work and to understand the importance of this service to humanity.

7 – *When an inexperienced counselor substitutes an experienced one, doesn't he or she risk being unable to deal with certain spirits who require more skill, a crafty obsessor for instance?*
► Rarely. Spirit mentors usually bring spirits who are compatible with the counselor's ability to the meeting. There is a tendency to bring only suffering spirits who need mostly kindness and attention to meetings that have inexperienced counselors.

8 – *Can mediums direct mediumistic meetings?*
▶ Yes, provided they don't perform both roles during a meeting. They must work either as mediums or coordinators. We need to consider, however, that a medium has difficulty in directing because he or she isn't able to avoid getting involved as a medium, and this compromises the efficiency of the work.

Simultaneous Counseling

1 – *What can you tell us about groups that do simultaneous counseling, i.e., helping two spirits or more at the same time?*
▶ When we consider that energetic harmony must prevail during any interaction with the beyond; it seems to me that it's an inconvenience. How do support people, the ones who provide fluidic support, behave with regard to the attention they need to pay? It's like being in a room trying to follow the conversations of three or four groups. We lose ourselves.

2 – *It's claimed that there's a possibility to help more spirits and give more opportunities to mediums this way.*
▶ If there are several mediums, obviously, there are several counselors for simultaneous counseling to take place. In that case, the group should be divided into two or three teams and work separately. There would be a better utilization of time.

3 – *What if the problem is available space? What if the center has only one room for the meeting?*
▶ This type of problem isn't usually the case. Usually, there are always other rooms that can be used. However, if this is a problem the same room can be used on alternate days.

4 – *Let's say, hypothetically, that the center only has one room and that all participants can only come at the same time.*

▶ It's a remote probability. But, if it happens, they should do simultaneous counseling, while being aware of the lack of efficiency due to the difficulties noted here.

5 – If the team is small, with two or three mediums, wouldn't simultaneous work be more efficient so that more spirits can benefit?
▶ It's reasonable for a medium to communicate two or at the most three manifestations and help each spirit separately. This can be done during the time reserved for mediumistic practice without problems with regard to time.

6 – What if there aren't skilled coordinators to direct groups such as the ones suggested here?
▶ The main problem with the direction of mediumistic work is how the spirits are treated. If the participants are able to do this well, in groups that do simultaneous counseling, then directors can be trained for that.

7 – And what about the times when there's a relationship between two communicating spirits? They even talk to one another!
▶ That's different. There's no group division here. Everyone is following the same dialogue, including the counselor, in perfect harmony.

8 – Are there any observations about this subject from Kardec?
▶ I don't know. But I believe that there's explicit guidance about this subject, when the codifier said in Chapter XXIX, item 341 from *The Spirits' Book*: *concentration and respectful silence during the interviews with the spirits.*
This concentration is difficult to attain when several incarnate and discarnate spirits talk at the same time.

Timetable

1 – It's said that a mediumistic meeting has a time to start but not to end. Is it true?
▶ It's a mistaken aphorism which complicates the work. If we want to have efficient and useful mediumistic meetings, we must have rules for everything we do. One of them is setting a time to start and end a meeting.

2 – Aren't the spirit mentors the ones who determine when it should end, depending on the number of entities to be helped?
▶ Spirit mentors who are experienced and knowledgeable also respect these rules. Obviously, in special circumstances the timetable can be slightly altered, but not significantly. If we do, there is a possibility that the discipline is compromised.

3 – What if a mentor extends the meeting routinely, asserting the need to help suffering entities?
▶ We must doubt the wisdom of such a practice and reflect on the inconveniences. It's even appropriate to evaluate the mentor. Mentors should know, better than anyone else, that discipline must be observed.

4 – What is the ideal time for a mediumistic meeting to last?
▶ Experience has shown that it should last between one hour and a half to one hour and forty five minutes, maximum 2 hours. When we exceed these limits, we can rarely maintain concentration, which is fundamental for the good results of the work. On the other hand, nothing prevents us from reducing the time to around half an hour and that is what happens with new groups.

5 – If five or more mediums are present, wouldn't it make sense to extend the time so that everyone may take care of their tasks?

▶ The number of manifestations must be restricted to the available time. If there are several mediums then they should have one manifestation each. If there are many, the group should be divided in two.

6 – *What if a medium feels the need to give more manifestations after filling his or her quota or after running out of time?*
▶ It's up to the spiritual mentors to control this situation so that only exceptions occur; when there are pressing needs. If it happens frequently, then there is a problem with the medium. He or she must be counseled.

7 – *Sometimes the meetings are extended because the director waits for a mentor to manifest. Is this reasonable?*
▶ No, there might not be mediums in condition to receive a mentor. Mentors may think that it's not the right time either. Mentor's manifestations are gladly received but without creating special conditions or making them a requirement.

8 – *Some people think that the mentor of each medium should manifest. It would be a form of "psychic cleansing" after the contact with disturbed and disturbing spirits.*
▶ That's another case of mistaken advice. It's a basic requirement for mediums to learn how to attune with the entities without absorbing their unstable vibrations.

Procedure

1 – *What would be the ideal procedure for a mediumistic meeting?*
▶ It depends on the type of meeting. The most common, the developmental meeting, can be divided in two parts:

theory and practice. First, there is a study period followed by manifestations.

2 – Must there always be a study period?
▶ No doubt, without a study period it becomes difficult to maintain the awareness of the responsibility and develop the group's potential.

3 – What type of study?
▶ Two types of books must be part of the study period. One must be about mediumship and the other must have evangelical content. The first is used to perfect spirit interaction techniques; the second for moral improvements.

4 – Does the meeting's director do the study part?
▶ Everyone must participate, alternating reading and commenting. The exchange of ideas about the topic serves as a complement. As for the evangelical text, a book previously selected can be used with comments from the director.

5 – How long should the first part last?
▶ Thirty minutes is reasonable.

6 – And the second?
▶ About one hour. The energy work[8] must be done between the theoretical and practical parts. And at the end, after the prayer, the director presides over the exchange of information about the night's work thus completing one hour and forty minutes as mentioned before.

7 – Wouldn't the time spent on initial studying and exchanging

---

8   Translator's Note: Energy work will be discussed in subsequent chapters of this book.

of information at the end be better utilized during the practical portion of the meeting so that more spirits could be helped?
▶ We should not worry about the total number of spirits we help. We should be concerned with the quality of the benefit they receive. The study and evaluation periods are fundamental in providing this quality.

8 – And what about the participation of mediums?
▶ It depends on their availability. If there are three mediums, two manifestations for each would be reasonable. If there are two, they should be available three times, and the same with one medium. Generally speaking a medium should not exceed three manifestations unless there's a special circumstance.

Energy Work

1 – What is this energy work done at a Spiritist House?
▶ In its simplest expression, it's a remote pass[9]. The meeting's members concentrate on one person's name with the intent of promoting health and peace. A spotlight of vibrations is formed to create an authentic light bath. The results are formidable.

2 – How is it done?
▶ The director, or an appointed person, slowly reads the name, address, and age of the beneficiary, stopping for half a minute, more or less, in each item. The members of the group can imagine themselves with the person, administering passes, saying positive words, visualizing improvements for the symptoms and solutions for the person, or they can simply pray for the person.

---

9   Translator's Note: Also known as 'vibrations'.

3 – *Why is the person's address needed?*

▶ It works as a point of reference. It's helpful to have an idea about the person's age and also where the person is located. This helps people concentrate better and direct their energies. We must also consider that spirit mentors mobilize to assist in the work and we should give them this information to facilitate their work.

4 – *Who writes this information down?*

▶ At the Spiritist Center Love and Charity in Bauru, the person fills out a card that they obtain from the reception area. Also, team members may refer people who can benefit from this service.

5 – *Should the person who is benefiting from the service remain in a state of concentration at the time of the energy work?*

▶ It would be ideal. The person should be reading an edifying book and praying at the appointed time. This facilitates the assimilation of the resources that are pulled together in the person's favor. This advice should be given to all interested parties.

6 – *Is it necessary to have faith?*

▶ Without a doubt. It establishes the needed attunement between the focus of energy and the person. It's also necessary to consider the *merit* factor, which is as important as faith. The person may not even believe in God, but if he or she leads an honorable and dignified life, turned toward the good, the receptivity is excellent. One can reach an elevated energetic state and attunement more easily with love than with fervor.

7 – *What if this person has no knowledge of the resources being mobilized in his or her benefit?*

▶ The result is less satisfactory. However, if the problem is caused by a tormenting spirit in the person's home, we can attract the entity to a mediumistic meeting with the help of the spiritual mentors.

8 – *Would it manifest?*
▶ I have noticed that this happens quite frequently. It's an opportunity to talk to the spirit and try to modify its disposition. Usually, it's someone having difficulties in adjusting to spirit life, who became fixated in the family, and is subconsciously disturbing them.

Energy Work, still

1 – *Some Spiritist Centers have meetings totally dedicated to energy work. Is this the ideal?*
▶ I believe that it's such an important service that it should be part of mediumistic development, disobsession, spiritual assistance meetings, and healing. Everyone can and should participate in them. It's gratifying for those who do it and highly productive for the beneficiaries.

2 – *Still, wouldn't it be appropriate to have specialized teams?*
▶ Anything we do to help people is important. We must consider, however, that it's difficult to sustain vibrations for a long time. The ideal would be to distribute the requests among several teams and extend the service for five or ten minutes.

3 – *In what portion of the mediumistic meeting should the vibration service take place?*
▶ Experience has shown that the ideal time is right after the study period. The group is "alive" and attentive and has ample vibrating capacity at this point. This is fundamental for the success of the task.

4 – *Some teams do this vibration work at the end of their meeting.*

▶ It doesn't seem advisable to me. After the mediumistic work, the participants have spent one to one and a half hours engaged in intense concentration. This concentration isn't just "paying attention." Besides, the opportunity to attract the spirits who are disturbing the person being helped that night is lost.

5 – *Should energy work be repeated several times?*

▶ It depends on availability. If there are just a few names on the list, then it can be done. Usually one treatment is sufficient because spiritual benefactors mobilize and take over the case.

6 – *Can we vibrate for discarnate spirits?*

▶ Without a doubt and with excellent results. They're more sensitive in that state. Even in the case of suicide, a spirit who is in the spirit world in painful perispiritual disarray feels a real relief for their torments.

7 – *Wouldn't it be better also to write down the nature of the problem so that the team's vibrations can be better directed?*

▶ It's not recommended because we must respect the person's privacy, especially when the reason for the request is behavioral problems. There's also the possibility of conditioning. The mediums may get involved with the problem and facilitate animism in the event that there's a manifestation.

8 – *Is it possible to do energy work alone, outside of a mediumistic meeting?*

▶ Yes, and we all do it frequently in spite of being unaware of it. Every time we pray for someone we send them good vibrations together with the blessings that come from heaven for the person.

Preparation

1 – Why is it stressed that we need to be in good physical and psychic condition in order to participate in meetings?

► It's because, in mediumistic work, the productivity and efficiency depend on maintaining the fluidic levels contributed by participants. It's necessary to meet these requirements so that a compatible standard of vibrations can be established.

2 – Is there any special preparation, with regard to thoughts, foods, and behavior?

► The idea of maintaining one perfect day for a mediumistic meeting is not the ideal. Our patterns of vibration aren't sustained by occasional care. It's necessary to be careful all the time.

3 – A practice for every day.

► Every moment! I don't see these principles as a faucet that can be turned on and off. Today I have a mediumistic meeting and, therefore, I'm careful with my food, and I control my thoughts and weaknesses. Our patterns of vibration are the sum of what we think and do at all times, not on concentrating for just a short while.

4 – If we consider that only saints can think and act for the good all the time, what can we do to improve our participation at least on the day of the meeting?

► We must set out, from the moment we wake up, to maintain serenity and to remember that we're going to be tempted in several circumstances. We must remember that irritability and aggressiveness are thoughts and feelings that aren't compatible with the commitments we made. Jesus taught that we must "pray and be vigilant."

5 – With regard to foods, is it reasonable to fast and consume

47

liquids only?
► There's nothing to prevent us from eating normally on meeting days. But we must be frugal. It's difficult to sustain concentration when the stomach is overly full. Concentration is one of the fundamentals of mediumistic work.

6 – Why is it that, particularly on meeting days, we come across all kinds of problems, especially at home?
► As we mentioned before, there are always spirits who are against our participation in any work that frees us from their influence. So they try to create problems; they influence people around us in order to reach us. This happens especially when we join a mediumistic group; it's the activity that bothers them the most.

7 – And how do we overcome this problem?
► The only way is to see them as tests we need to face calmly and with a good disposition. If we persevere in our good intentions, these spirits do, eventually, give up and recognize that the pressure they exert isn't yielding any effect.

8 – If we have difficulties during the day and allow ourselves to be controlled by thoughts and feelings that aren't compatible with mediumistic work, would it be reasonable not to attend and admit that we're not in condition to do so?
► If we do that, we'll give up eventually. Fundamentally, what is asked of us is that we don't slack; don't stop fighting our weaknesses. So as long we do this, we'll have the protection of our spirit friends; they'll try to help us overcome our difficulties.

Animism

1 – *What is animism?*
▶ In mediumistic practices, it's when the medium's soul interferes with the spirit interaction. Kardec used the term somnambulism; he explained in *Posthumous Work,* Item 46: Somnambulists act under the influence of their own spirit; their souls are the ones that, in moments of emancipation, hear and perceive beyond sensory limits. What is expressed, then, comes from the medium.

2 – *Is animism always present in manifestations?*
▶ A medium is not a telephone. The medium captures the entity's mental waves and transmits them using his or her own resources. There is always something of the medium in the transmission, particularly if the medium is a beginner and has difficulty in discerning between what is his or hers and what comes from the spirit.

3 – *Is there a percentage of animism in every communication? Let's say forty percent from the medium and sixty percent from the spirit?*
▶ Animism is part of the process, we can say that there's always a percentage but it's not a fixed number. It varies depending on the medium's development. Usually neophytes put more of themselves in the communication. When they're experienced mediums they tend to interfere less.

4 – *Could there be a manifestation completely animistic without the medium's knowledge?*
▶ It's a common thing; it happens when the medium is stressed and finding difficulty in coping with personal problems. Emotions have a tendency to interfere, and the medium ends up transmitting some of his or her own anxieties in a supposed manifestation.

5 – *Would it be mystification?*

▶ No, because there is no intent. The medium isn't trying to deceive anyone. The medium is a victim of his or her own maladjustments and is not aware of what is happening.

6 – *And what should the meeting's directors do when they notice that a team member is doing this?*

▶ One must be careful! An inexperienced director may see animism where there isn't any. If experience indicates that it's really happening, the director must talk to the medium in private. The group's lead must try to find out if there are personal problems and guide the person through spiritual treatment. If the problem persists, the medium must be advised to participate in the meeting as a support member only and avoid mediumistic manifestations.

7 – *If animism is more noticeable in beginners, what should the director do when they're leading a developing team?*

▶ Usually, only suffering spirits come to these meetings, those experiencing problems adapting to spirit life and those who aren't aware of their situation. In these circumstances, the director doesn't need to worry about animism in manifestations. The director should simply help the entities who manifest. It's necessary to take the time to guide mediums in their studies so that they can overcome these initial difficulties.

8 – *When should a director worry about animism?*

▶ When a mentor manifests. It's necessary to use the litmus test to identify not only animism, but also mystification from the communicating spirit.

Concentration

1 – What is concentration?
► It's the convergence of thoughts for a predetermined goal. In its simplest expression, it's to pay attention.

2 – Why does a director ask for better concentration several times?
► Concentration is the first rule to be observed. They must be attentive from the moment that the meeting starts, attentive to what is going on.

3 – What if the participants are distracted?
► They would be affecting the good results of the meeting. Kardec says in *The Mediums' Book* [10]: *"A meeting is a collective being, whose qualities and properties are the sum of all of its members, forming a sort of cluster, and this cluster will be stronger the more homogenous it is"* Furthermore, *"If a spirit is in any way struck by thought – as we are by voice, then twenty individuals united with the same intent will obviously have more power than only one. However, in order for all thoughts to contribute toward the same goal, they must vibrate in unison and blend themselves into single thought, something that cannot occur without concentration."*

4 – Is it necessary to close our eyes?
► During prayers, yes, if the person feels better this way. If the person isn't praying they may keep their eyes open and follow the proceedings. When eyes are closed there's a tendency to disconnect, thoughts are far away, predisposed to sleep. I've seen sleepy heads that even snore and cause embarrassment for others.

---

10   The Mediums' Book: Part Two, Chapter XXIX, Item 331 (International Spiritist Council – First Edition – 2007)

5 – *There are people who say that this is detachment. The soul is taken away to collaborate from the spiritual side. They say also that while asleep the person is providing fluidic resources that help the meeting.*

▶ We cannot deny the gift of imagination in people who say these things. It's a good try; to treat sleepy heads as participants. If this idea catches perhaps, many people will try to 'collaborate' by sleeping through the meeting.

6 – *What is the ideal attitude for a medium?*

▶ During the study period and initial comments, the medium should be attentive and interested in everything. When the mediumistic work starts and spirits' presences are felt, they should close their eyes. They should try to connect with the energy in the environment and the being who is influencing them. This provides the best mental conditions for manifestations to occur.

7 – *What about the counselor? Should he or she also keep their eyes closed?*

▶ If the person prefers they may keep their eyes closed while counseling. There are directors that feel more receptive to the spirits this way. The effort of speaking will keep them awake and attentive.

8 – *Considering that to concentrate is to pay attention, should the support members be continuously attentive throughout the entire meeting?*

▶ Yes and they can improve their participation by "talking" to the disturbed or disturbing spirits who manifest. They should direct words of kindness and caring thoughts to them. They must try to envelop the spirit in beneficial vibrations which may help the counselor's work. This sometimes is more efficient than counseling.

Purposeful Illnesses

1 – Should a sick medium avoid coming to the meeting?
▶ It depends on the type of problem. If it's a bad cold, with fever, it's better to miss the meeting so that the others don't get sick also. There are however, physical and psychic symptoms that come from a suffering spirit. Often spiritual mentors bring them over so that an initial contact may facilitate the manifestation that will take place later.

2 – In this case, even if the medium doesn't feel well, he or she should attend?
▶ Yes, because what the medium is feeling is part of the work. The medium is feeling the anguish and sensations the spirit is feeling. The symptoms are related to the illness or problems the spirit felt when in the physical life.

3 – This means that a pain in the leg, for instance, can be of a spiritual origin?
▶ It's common. It happens especially with a medium of greater sensitivity. When a medium transmits the manifestation of a spirit because of circulatory problems and there was gangrene on the leg, the medium usually feels a similar pain before the meeting, due to the proximity of the entity.

4 – The same occurs with emotions?
▶ It's common. When a medium connects with a spirit, he or she feels what is going on with the spirit. If the entity is tormented, afflicted, tense, nervous or anguished the medium feels some of these emotions.

5 – What if the medium thinks that these physical and emotional symptoms come from their own lives and decides not to come to the meeting?
▶ If we have been trusted with the task of taking a person

to a hospital but we decide to keep the patient at home with us instead, we'll be taking the responsibility of caring for the person. Certainly, the patient will be a lot of trouble for us, especially if it's a mental patient.

6 – *Is it possible that this connection with disturbed entities takes place independently of a spiritual mentor's initiatives?*
▶ It's what happens most of the time. We're constantly surrounded by panic-stricken spirits who have no knowledge of spirit life. They grab on to people the same way that victims of a shipwreck grab on to a floating piece of wood. It's not necessary to be an ostensive medium. We all run this risk.

7 – *Let's say that a medium feels this kind of influence on Monday and the meeting is on Saturday. Must they suffer for the entire week?*
▶ As mediums study and gain experience they learn to deal with this problem. They pray and talk quietly with the entity who then is helped with assistance from spirit mentors.

8 – *Should we tell this to people who seek help from the center and are disturbed by such entities?*
▶ We must be careful. There are vulnerable persons who are mistaken about demoniac influences; they may panic. They'll never set foot in a Spiritist Center again. We've seen this happen, because of people's ineptitude.

Obstacles

1 – *Mediumistic meeting directors complain about the team's inconsistent attendance. They say that members are rarely present all at the same time. Does this hinder the work?*
▶ No doubt. When the participants create harmony with

54

respect to the meeting's objectives, the team forms what we call a "mediumistic body." Absenteeism breaks the potential for an effective meeting.

2 – *If a specific spirit is set to manifest through a certain medium and the medium isn't at the meeting, can another medium substitute?*
▶ Yes, but without the desired efficiency; we must consider that a manifestation requires harmony between entity and medium, which is usually accomplished before the meeting. If, after a preliminary contact, the medium is absent, the work is hindered.

3 – *There are directors who suspend mediums from the work. The consequence of one missed meeting is one meeting in which he or she is not allowed to work. If they miss two, they will serve as support for two. Is this reasonable?*
▶ I don't know of any doctrinal basis for this behavior; it seems to me more like punishment than discipline. Before we impose restrictions we should talk to the person and explain how important his or her presence is. When people feel appreciated they serve better; they're diligent with their commitments.

4 – *Isn't this in conflict with the advice that some directors give that one should never compliment or value a medium's work to avoid flattery?*
▶ They certainly don't know the effect a good word has. To encourage a team member by recognizing their merit is a valuable reinforcement. Obviously, we shouldn't be artificial, like a certain director who used to say: *You are the light that illuminates our meeting! The rock that sustains our work!* Easy and theatrical flattery sounds ridiculous and empty.

5 – *What is the ideal approach for people not to neglect their spiritual commitments?*

▶ Our dear Spiritist friend Homero Escobar, already deceased, used to say wisely: *"The best way to meet our spiritual commitments is to treat them like our professional commitments."*

6 – *Does this mean we should be absent only for imperative reasons?*

▶ Exactly. If it's raining and we have to go to work we use an umbrella. If it's cold we wear our coats. If we have a visitor we ask them to excuse us. If the car breaks down we take a bus or a taxi. If we treat our spiritual obligations differently; any of these situations will stop us. It shouldn't be this way. After all, our job ensures physical survival but spiritual activity nourishes our souls. It's how we qualify for protection from spirit benefactors.

7 – *Isn't the lack of seriousness in tending to spiritual commitments the reason that mediumistic meetings suffer reductions in size?*

▶ It happens, unfortunately. We must recognize however, that there are other reasons. People's lives change. I've seen people leave because they started a course of study, because they moved, because of a new family commitment, or because of changes in their working hours.

8 – *What should be done when the team is reduced?*

▶ It depends on who stays. A team can work with only five or six persons, counting mediums and counselors, as long as they're all serious to attendance and dedication. Nothing stops directors, however, from inviting other people, properly prepared, to join the meeting.

Psychography

1 – *Does the exercise of psychography, or channel writing, require a specialized mediumistic meeting?*
▶ Psychography is a unique mediumistic ability. If the medium attends to the discipline and is well trained, it can be done in any type of meeting.

2 – *At home also?*
▶ Yes, mediums who publish their work establish an appropriate time to write, usually in their own homes. If we consider that the spirits also have commitments and are not at our disposal we can see that every mediumistic activity requires discipline. That's how we're able to count on them, be it at home or at the Spiritist Center.

3 – *Isn't it complicated for a medium to maintain the needed concentration when there are manifestations going on at a meeting?*
▶ Maybe in principle, but with practice the medium can isolate elements in the environment and concentrate his or her mind on the flow of thoughts that come from the communicating spirit.

4 – *Is it reasonable to expect, in a developmental meeting, that every participant try automatic writing?*
▶ In principle, this ability entails an impulse to write. Therefore, there should be a subject to write about. Usually, when this faculty needs to be developed, spirit mentors release it.

5 – *Is a psychographer simply a medium who writes instead of articulating the spirit's thoughts?*
▶ We could say so. There's a certain correlation between the variants. A mechanical channel writer is equivalent to

an unconscious trance medium, a semi-mechanic to a semi-conscious, and an intuitive to a conscious. There are mediums who do both.

6 – Should the work of a psychographic medium be disseminated and eventually published in books?
▶ Students learning the basics of writing should not expect to publish their first attempts. It's the same with mediums who start to channel write. The person is starting a task that, usually matures in a future life.

7 – This explains why we have so many weak mediumistic books, from the literary as much as the doctrinal point of view.
▶ Unfortunately, it happens with simple exercises. Often, a medium is encouraged by cohorts who stir up his or her vanity. They become convinced that they were selected for a special task and insist on having their writings published. They publish books that do not contribute anything. They're imitations of Spiritist literature.

8 – Should Spiritist publishers use rigorous criteria in evaluating the manuscripts they receive to stop this from happening?
▶ Usually, they're careful. However, it's easy to publish books nowadays, with modern publishing resources and data processing wonders available at home. Hence, the proliferation of bad books; usually authors or groups publish them.

Seeing Mediums

1 – How should we define seeing mediums?
▶ As it happens often in our language, the term 'seeing' has several meanings. A seeing medium is a person who can see

with their eyes. It's also a person who sees the future, one who sees distances far away, or a sharp person. In the Spiritist context, it's a person who sees the spirit world.

2 – People who are disturbed and have difficult lives or health problems can sometimes see the spirit world. Is this a faculty that can be developed?
► Not necessarily. As with any other faculty that involves the spirit world the person may be able to see because of a psychic super excitement. After they undergo spiritual treatment, the faculty disappears.

3 – It's common that terminally ill patients report seeing their departed family members. Doctors say that it's hallucination caused by weakness. Is it?
► Conventional medicine feels its way around, always opting for 'reducing' explanations, that is, it reduces everything to phenomena that involve the brain. What happens is that, when the ties that bind the terminal patient to the spiritual body loosen, the person's perception is heightened. As a result the person has visions of dead relatives. Ordinarily, the loved ones are helping them return to spirit life. Stephen, the first Christian martyr, experienced this phenomenon. When he expired, his spiritual vision was opened to him. As he was being stoned, he perceived the presence of Jesus, who had come to assist him.

4 – Can anyone develop this seeing ability?
► It's possible, with proper training, and specific disciplines and exercises to learn the basics. Still, for the phenomenon to occur in a more intense way, it's necessary that the faculty be present.

5 – A medium describes a great waterfall, a large river, or a group of horsemen. How can these images be formed in the meeting room?

▶ There are two types of seeing abilities, the objective and the subjective. The subjective one appears in the medium's mind as ideoplastic or idealized scenes. So when someone says that he or she can see these visions, it's because something was formed in their mental screen.

6 – *What's the use of this type of seeing?*

▶ They respond to ideas that spirit mentors suggest. The mediums give form according to his or her knowledge and culture, with richness of details. They're symbolisms for the group to interpret.

7 – *And objective seeing?*

▶ The medium sees the spirit world and the spirits present. In a more advanced stage, the medium can see with opened eyes without concentrating or being in a trance. Jesus had this faculty. We see him talking to tormenting spirits in several Evangelical passages as he orders them to leave their victims. Chico Xavier also had this ability; he used to communicate messages from discarnate beings to their families who would be present in the meeting.

8 – *Would it be helpful to have a seeing medium in a meeting to help the counselor?*

▶ It becomes very complicated, considering that the majority of seeing is subjective. Even those who have objective seeing can often make mistakes because of crafty spirits. Interference from a seeing medium may confuse the counselor. It's better to discuss what the seeing medium saw during the evaluation period. As for the counselor, the best source of information is intuition, knowledge and experience.

Incorporation or Trance Communication[11]

1 – What is mediumship of incorporation?
▶ Although the term has been established by common use, it's wrong. It suggests that the manifesting spirit enters the medium's body in order to transmit its thoughts; this doesn't happen. Our body is inalienable; it's not liable to be substituted or host another spirit. At most, we can say that the medium 'incorporates' the entity's ideas, impressions and sensations.

2 – What is the correct term?
▶ Kardec used speaking mediums; it didn't catch in Brazil. We use the term psychophony which is also incorrect; it suggests that the medium's soul is speaking, which is something closer to animism. Nevertheless, incorporation, as well as psychophony or trance-communication, has been established by use.

3 – Do all psychophonic or trance mediums work the same way?
▶ Obviously. All of them transmit spirits' thoughts through their own articulated words. The difference is in the depth of the mediumistic trance. Thus, we can divide psychophony into three types: conscious, semi-conscious, and unconscious.

4 – How can we distinguish them?
▶ A conscious medium is awake as the spirit's thoughts are perceived and transmitted. An unconscious medium is in a deeper trance and moves away from the body so that the spirit

---

11   Translator Note: Incorporation is the literal translation of the word in Portuguese. In English speaking countries the term used is trance communication or psychophony.

can communicate in a more direct way, as though there was a true incorporation. As for the semi-conscious medium he or she has a little of both types. The trance isn't deep enough to produce unconsciousness, nor so superficial to keep the medium completely awake. Using a rough comparison we might say that the conscious medium thinks before speaking; the unconscious speaks without thinking, and the semi-conscious thinks and speaks simultaneously.

5 – *Why is unconscious psychophony more authentic and more rare?*
▶ It's occurrence is more adequate but also more problematic. Generally speaking, the medium falls asleep at the beginning of the meeting and wakes up at the end without any involvement with or obligation to the mediumistic work. If the person is not careful, he or she can be driven by mystifying spirits.

6 – *They don't control the manifestations?*
▶ They can. However, if the medium isn't careful about responsibilities and is not fully integrated in the mediumistic work, he or she can stay in a torpor that inhibits the possibility of control.

7 – *Is the semi-conscious medium the ideal?*
▶ There is no ideal type of medium. There are ideal mediums; they're the ones who are aware of the responsibilities and face the commitments inherent to this type of work.

8 – *We notice that nowadays the majority of mediums are conscious. Is this a growing tendency?*
▶ Yes, although there are more difficulties, this type of medium fares better. Conscious psychophony requires more study, discipline, and inner transformation, which facilitates a better transmission whether they're from obsessors, suffering

spirits or mentors.

Initial difficulties

1 – *How does conscious mediumship work?*
► The medium attunes to the spirit's mental flux. Then, ideas
and/or sensations are created as though another mind interferes
with the medium's thoughts, or they're talking to someone
inside their own heads.

2 – *Can they hear voices?*
► It would be easier if they did, but that's not how it really
is. Ideas appear mixing with one's own, as if they were one's
own.

3 – *It sounds complicated ...*
► It is, no doubt, especially for beginner mediums who
cannot distinguish what is theirs from what is the spirit's.
Many of them leave mediumistic practice because of this
disturbing uncertainty.

4 – *How can this problem be solved?*
► Mediums need to trust and let the ideas that come to mind
flow freely, even if they seem jumbled up at first. Usually,
mediums under development start with the manifestation
of suffering spirits and that makes the process simpler.
Connecting ideas or reasoning effort aren't required. In
principle, the only requirement is to transmit feelings and
sensations from the spirit.

5 – *What is your advice for a medium facing this challenge?*
► To start talking as soon as an independent flow of
sensations or thoughts are felt, without worrying if its theirs

or a spirit's. From that point on the flow self-adjusts. It's like an inexperienced driver. At first there are some jolts but soon everything becomes second nature.

6 – *What can be done to help novice mediums?*
► Help from the team is important; the medium is very fragile at this time. He or she feels vulnerable and embarrassed. Any hostility or criticism from team members affects the person adversely.

7 – *Would it be advisable to administer passes to new mediums to start the manifestation?*
► A pass may help but we should use it sparingly in order to avoid conditioning. There are mediums who wait for the coordinator to intervene with passes before they start to work.

8 – *Manifestations from new mediums are often repetitive. How should the meeting's coordinator act in this case?*
► Cultivate understanding and kindness; consider that animism and intervention from the medium are likely to occur at this phase of development. The medium will adjust slowly and will learn how to distinguish their ideas from the spirit's.

Giving up

1 – *Frequently, we see mediums with reasonable mediumistic faculties walk out on the commitment. Is there any harm?*
► Mediumistic sensitivity doesn't work only during mediumistic meetings. It's always present! It's in practicing it, studying it, and with discipline that the medium finds resources to sustain equilibrium. When they're away from it, mediums may fall into grave disturbances and maladjustments.

2 – *Is it punishment?*

▶ It's not about punishment. The problem is that the person's sensitivity, when it's not controlled by practice, places the medium at the mercy of negative influences and disturbing entities, wherever they may be.

3 – *Isn't this a problem in everyone's life? Aren't we surrounded by disturbed and disturbing spirits all the time?*

▶ Yes, and we know the problems that come up because people are completely ignorant on this subject. For a medium who is away from mediumistic work this problem is more serious. The sensitivity in mediums causes them to suffer a greater impact, with negative repercussions in the psyche.

4 – *What if the medium, although away from the work, is a good, compassionate, kind and well-balanced person?*

▶ Such a behavior can bring relative stability, but we need to consider that mediumship is not a biological accident. No one is born a medium without a reason. There are commitments inherent to it.

5 – *The medium is already programmed when he or she is born....*

▶ Yes. It's a commitment made in the spirit world. There's an investment of time and energy made by the candidate to mediumship, which is connected with studies, planning, and preparation of the body. All of it requires diligent care from spirit mentors. Imagine a company investing in an employee's training for a certain job. After all the work, is it reasonable for the employee to say that he's no longer interested?

6 – *But isn't it counter-productive for a person to participate in mediumship work, as someone tending to a duty or a pre-established contract, because of fear of sanctions?*

▶ The sanctions come from the person's own conscience; it

demands reparation sooner or later. Mediums should study Spiritism to avoid this situation; they should take courses and refresher courses in order to maintain their responsibilities in mediumistic work.

7 – What if there are reasonable obstacles? Children to care for, difficult spouse, job, health?
► This may happen for a while. The biggest problem however is when the medium tries to justify his or her omission. It's highly unlikely that the spirits would grant mediumship ability without the conditions to practice it.

8 – What about intransigent spouses creating problems for the medium at home?
► A marriage where the husband or wife wants to ruin the spouse's religious activity is regrettable indeed. It's inconceivable! Where are the communication, understanding, and respect for the other's convictions? Although this type of problem may justify a medium's absence, it doesn't exempt them from complications stemming from failed mediumistic work.

Participants

1 – What is the number of persons needed for a mediumistic meeting?
► Jesus said that when two or more met in his name, he would be there. In the same way we can say that contact with the spirit world is possible with two people with mediumistic psychophony ability. One medium and someone to talk to the spirits are enough. Chico Xavier worked for a while with his brother, Jose Xavier, who directed the work.

2 – *Isn't this an extremely low number?*

▶ No doubt, it should be an exception. When mediumistic meetings have the sustaining energy of a reasonable number of people the result is a better operation.

3 – *What number should we say is "reasonable"?*

▶ Eight to twenty members, appropriately prepared and conscientious of their responsibilities would be best.

4 – *Why should we set a limit? If a mediumistic meeting needs an energetic maintenance that is provided by the participants, wouldn't it be better to have a larger number? Fifty for instance?*

▶ Let's keep in mind the need for harmony in the team. It's necessary that members know each other well and empathize with one another. The larger the group the harder it is to achieve this harmony. There's a tendency for the team to be too heterogeneous.

5 – *In this line of thinking, it sounds like a one-digit number would be best, less than ten.*

▶ The ideal is always a reasonable number of people in harmony with each other. I've worked with groups of twenty persons without problems.

6 – *It takes time to harmonize a team of this size. How can this problem be overcome at the beginning?*

▶ As we have said, no one should participate in a mediumistic meeting without previous training. At our center we have a preparatory course that lasts two years. In the first year they teach the Spiritist Doctrine and basic topics including *The Spirits' Book* and *The Gospel According to Spiritism.* In the second year, they teach *The Mediums' Book.* At the end, the class has a good understanding and is in step with the purpose and responsibilities of the meeting.

7 – Beyond this preparation, what else can be done to help the team's harmonization?

▶ An old spirit mentor used to advise the workers to volunteer for charitable work at the center, which involved attending to needy persons. The objective: to improve the energy level by practicing the greater good. The ideal would be that the entire team takes up a common commitment.

8 – What if a team member does not have the time to participate in any activity?

▶ Time is a question of preference. We always find time to do what we think is important. Not finding time for work that helps needy people means the person doesn't understand the Spiritist message.

Materializations

1 – How is spirit materialization done in meetings of physical effects?

▶ The term is inadequate; spirits don't materialize. They use ectoplasm, which is a substance the medium excretes, to cover themselves. In a bad comparison, it's as though an invisible man painted his entire body so that we could see him.

2 – Why are meetings of physical effects, where materializations take place, rare in Spiritist Centers?

▶ According to our spirit mentors, the time for ostensive phenomena is over. We must now care for humanity's dematerialization in the sense of helping them relinquish excessive attachment to immediate interests.

3 – Is this in order to favor doctrinal studies?

▶ Yes, the emphasis should be on moral orientation, trying to overcome our weaknesses, and renouncing personal interests for the common good.

4 – *Aren't these phenomena extremely efficient in demonstrating survival of the soul and the possibility of interaction?*
► When we can count on a well prepared medium, they're spectacular but tend to work as fireworks. They create enthusiasm and go away. Even when they provide elements to convince someone of immortality, they rarely make a difference in an individual's behavior, in a moral sense. They don't help people become more aware of their responsibilities toward an immortal life, where God's justice is never absent.

5 – *In spite of this, wouldn't it be reasonable for a center to develop this kind of work, considering that they're part of the mediumistic process and are mentioned in the Spiritist codification?*
► No doubt, there's nothing against it. It's even opportune to have co-workers busy with phenomena such as these. What happens is that just a few mediums are of the physical effect type. This shows that the direction of Spiritism of today, under the guidance of spirit mentors, is different.

6 – *Often, people seek out a Spiritist Center because they're frightened by some phenomenon that happened in their houses: lights, sounds, apparitions, malfunctions in electrical or electronic equipment which seem to happen because of spirit influence. Isn't this an opportunity for physical effect mediums who could be used for physical effects meetings?*
► When we analyze these occurrences, we usually find out that they have nothing to do with spirit influence. They're natural phenomena, interpreted wrongly or they're products of the imagination.

7 – What if they really are happening?

▶ In this case, we are in the presence of a medium who needs to be oriented and supported with resources offered Spiritism so he can deal with such phenomena.

8 – Do mediums develop physical effect abilities?

▶ Only time can tell. It's necessary to frequent a center, attend meetings, study Spiritism and mediumship. If there's a commitment with mediumship, it'll be verified in the practice.

Mediumistic Prescriptions

1 – There are several Spiritist Centers that dispense mediumistic prescriptions[12]. Does it require a special kind of mediumship?

▶ A prescription medium is an automatic writer who has specialized in this mediumistic area. He or she can write messages as well as prescriptions.

2 – Would it be better to avoid this service considering that the medium may be liable to law suits or illegal medical practices, for instance?

▶ It could happen but it's doubtful. Consider that discarnate doctors prescribe; it would be strange to include them in a law suit. They're still doctors, although in the beyond, with knowledge and experience they acquired on earth.

3 – It happens that human justice doesn't provide for the

---

12   Translator's Note: The author refers to procedures followed by many Spiritist Centers in Brazil. Each country has its specific legislation to be followed on this regard.

survival of the spirit and that makes this reasoning invalid.

▶ The fact that the law doesn't accept that spirit doctors are writing the prescriptions clashes with the Spiritist Doctrine's faith whose teachings say it is possible. Can the law persecute a priest for illegal practice of medicine when he gives holy water to heal body and soul?

4 – Holy water is different from prescribed medicine. Drugs can be prescribed wrongly and cause harm to the patient.

▶ This can happen with medicine from earth; it's highly unlikely to happen with medicine from Heaven unless we're dealing with inexperienced or mystifying mediums. It's up to the Spiritist director to take the necessary precautions.

5 – Would it be advisable to evaluate the results with the patients?

▶ No doubt. It's important also to verify the medium's efficiency, as well as the discarnate doctor's. As it should be with any professional field, it's necessary to evaluate the results to see if the service can be continued.

6 – We notice that mediumistic prescriptions usually involve homeopathy and phytology. Is there a special reason?

▶ It's used precisely to avoid the medium's involvement with the illegal practice of medicine. They're simplified therapeutic practices that act mildly on the organism without the complexity of allopathic medicine. It's easier for the medium to become familiar with the therapy.

7 – Should a Spiritist Center encourage this activity?

▶ If there are mediums capable of being efficient in this practice, yes. It seems to me that it's an excellent resource in human health, especially in our country where health care for the poor is precarious, particularly when it comes to paying for medicine.

71

8 – *If mediumistic prescription is acceptable, wouldn't it also be advisable to adopt color and crystal therapies, life regression, and others?*
▶ Without mentioning their merits, which are real, they have nothing to do with mediumistic practices. It's advisable that they be practiced outside a Spiritist Center by specialists.

Healing Mediums

1 – *What is the difference between healing mediums and pass-givers who administer magnetic passes?*
▶ The same difference that separates a surgeon from a general clinician. The pass is a 'clinical' treatment. An intervention from a healing medium, when it's necessary, is 'surgery'.

2 – *There are healing mediums who use surgical instruments, knives, and scissors. Others use only the imposition of hands as though they were giving a pass. Why this difference?*
▶ It's a question of methodology and mediumistic specialization. When a healing medium uses the imposition of hands the intervention is on the perispirit, where the focus of maladjustment that causes physical illness usually resides. If healing is possible with the magnetic treatment, the repercussion will take place quickly in the body and the cure happens.

3 – *What is the difference between the healing medium doing laying-on-of-hands and the pass-giver who is a member of a team for magnetic healing? Isn't it the same process?*
▶ The pass-giver is a donor of magnetic energy. The healing medium provides energy which is, let's say, more dense. It's what is called ectoplasm; it provides a more intense action in favor of the patient.

4 – Which method is more correct? Surgical instruments or hands?

▶ The question isn't methodology, but authenticity. If it's serious work, and if the medium is honest, detached, and dedicated, the results are satisfactory with either method.

5 – If you needed a healing medium, which method would you choose?

▶ Spiritual surgery. It's not spectacular; it's less invasive and more efficient. It reaches deeply into what is wrong, in the perispirit. Intervention by surgical instruments is about effects on the body.

6 – Do you have anything against surgical mediums?

▶ No. I even understand that, if the medium is authentic and well assisted, notable therapeutic effects can take place, but nothing that exceeds, in efficiency, a good surgeon. However, interventions on the perispirit go beyond the possibilities of conventional medicine. It's the ideal field for mediumistic assistance.

7 – What about karma? Is it possible, in spiritual surgery, to heal serious maladies that have been planned and determined to cause the patient to die?

▶ Yes, if spirit mentors think it's convenient to grant a 'moratorium' for a righteous reason or to complete a specific task. I've seen it happen, with cases of expansion of up to twenty years.

8 – It happens that people who benefit from spiritual treatment come back after a while with the same problem. Would this be karma?

▶ It could be. It's more correct however, to say that our maladies are related to our deficiencies. If we want something beyond palliative care we need to remember what Jesus used to say when he healed: *Go and sin no more, so that nothing worse happens to you.*

The Nature of the Meetings

1 – What determines the type of meeting a center has?
▶ Intention and aptitude. The Center's directors plan the type of mediumistic work that they wish to develop, but always dependent on the group's availability. It would be useless to plan for a materialization meeting without physical effect mediums.

2 – Wouldn't it be better if this orientation came from the spirits?
▶ Yes, provided there are mediums who are able to channel or transmit messages from spirit mentors who can be trusted. Once, at a mediumistic meeting that I directed, a spirit manifested saying he was a doctor. He informed us that he was beginning a prescription service. I explained to him that this work would be completely outside the purposes for a new team. He never showed up again.

3 – What is the ideal work for beginners?
▶ Experience has shown that new teams work with suffering spirits brought over to be helped. The contact is easier with those who are still linked to physical impressions. They also don't demand much effort from a medium, who transmits the spirit's emotions and sensations, considering that they don't have much to say because they're in crisis.

4 – According to this point of view, could we say that mediumistic teams evolve toward other types of work?
▶ It's what usually happens, although it depends on the

availability of mediums. Regardless of how much it develops, a team will never specialize in mediumistic prescriptions, if there are no able mediums.

5 – There are teams that work for years without great progress. They work with suffering spirits and no manifestations from spirit mentors. Why is that?
▶ It's because of the team's lack of effort. It's necessary to study and improve oneself, modify habits, improve the vibration standards, grow spiritually. This is especially true with regard to mediums; if they don't follow these directives they rarely provide the conditions needed to work in disobsession or for transmitting the communications of spirit mentors.

6 – If the team stagnates, is the work lost?
▶ Lost, no. There are always benefits when we decide to work. It may be precarious and deficient. But this happens in any type of activity. The one who makes more effort produces more and makes more progress.

7 – Are disobsession meetings an evolutionary step for a mediumistic group?
▶ Every mediumistic meeting that assists discarnate beings works with disobsession even when they're new. Usually, we find *peaceful obsession*; that's when spirits who passed on recently torment their families. They're attached to them and don't realize that they're in the spirit world. As the team grows, becomes more knowledgeable, and has a larger sense of responsibility, the contacts with difficult spirits happen; i.e. those bent on revenge, evil, addictions, etc.

8 – We can conclude that mediumistic teams must not be static, but dynamic, always improving, and trying to expand the possibilities provided by the interaction.

▶ Exactly. We must not miss the blessed opportunity for edifying work that mediumship makes possible. Teams that aren't interested in studying end up working as amateurs without greater commitments; they lag behind. Usually, they dissolve because of lack of motivation or because of influence from the spirits who don't want this kind of practice which can neutralize their influence on others.

Meetings in the Home

1 – How can mediumistic meetings be done outside of a Spiritist Center?
▶ We can do surgery outside of a hospital, but it's always risky; it's the same with a mediumistic meeting. The appropriate place is a Spiritist Center, where the spirits mobilize adequate resources for best results.

2 – What are the problems with holding mediumistic meetings in the home?
▶ Besides not being the appropriate place, there's the danger of attracting tormenting spirits who may feel that spiritual assistance endangers them, or disturbed spirits who come to the house looking for help. In a Spiritist Center the work is impersonal; it's not centralized on a person or persons, and the workers are safer. The institution is the head.

3 – What if one of the workers at the Spiritist Center is sick and cannot come to the meeting; isn't it advisable, in this case, to have the meeting in his or her home?
▶ There are exceptions. If the plan is to help the worker with a message from a mentor, then it's all right. However, it's when exceptions become routine and the group gets used to holding meetings in homes that problems may arise. This

happens frequently.

4 – What should we think of mediums who see people in their homes and go into a trance to receive a mentor?
▶ They take unnecessary risks and attract spirits who may exploit their weaknesses, usually inducing them to commercialize their faculties. They then charge for services or accept gifts. They're better off submitting to the disciplines of a Spiritist Center which protects them from their own bad tendencies.

5 – Usually the Spiritist Movement starts with a small group meeting in people's homes. Is it justified since they don't have a Spiritist Center in which to meet?
▶ Nothing prevents us from forming a group of interested persons and meeting at home to study Spiritism. It's when we try to transform a home study meeting into mediumistic work that we begin to have problems.

6 – If having a mediumistic meeting at home is a problem, why is it done in Spiritist circles?
▶ Because many people are not interested in studying Spiritism; they develop mediumistic practices that are not compatible with doctrinal orientation. For instance, often they ask for spiritual advice in these meetings. They forget that this is not the reason for interactions with the beyond.

7 – Wouldn't the presence of spirit benefactors, if the meeting is held at a center, a desired sign of approval?
▶ Responsible and knowledgeable spirit mentors certainly guide the group to meet at a Spiritist Center.

8 – What if a spirit benefactor gives another type of guidance, encouraging the activity to take place at the medium's home or at the home of another team member?

▶ It's time, as Kardec advises, to question the source. Is it really a spirit mentor? It could, perhaps, be a familiar spirit, one who has good will, but is lacking in discernment. Spirit mentors emphasize that we should always practice it in a Spiritist Center: our temple, our workshop, our blessed school.

Physical Environment

1 – Is it necessary to turn off the lights to do mediumistic work?
▶ Only in meeting of physical effects. It's because ectoplasm, the substance provided by the medium to produce the phenomena, is sensitive to light.

2 – There are Spiritist Centers that turn the lights off at every mediumistic meeting.
▶ They're careless. Light has no bearing on interactions and it's interesting for the members to observe the mediums and their reactions as they transmit the communications. We can, if everyone feels more comfortable, dim the lights.

3 – What is the table's purpose in mediumistic meetings?
▶ Nothing makes it indispensable; we can perform interactive work without it. At times, it would be more practical for the entire team to make a circle.

4 – Traditionally, whenever we think of the physical environment for a mediumistic meeting, the first thing that comes to mind is the table. Wouldn't it be strange to eliminate it?
▶ It's only an accessory. What is strange is that a mediumistic team becomes dependent on it, thus making it indispensable.

5 – Should the participants follow the practice of using the so called 'captive chair' and always sit in the same place?
► We do it because of habit. It shouldn't be imperative because it doesn't mean anything for the continuity of the meeting. It's not important where we sit; it's important to participate in the correct manner, being attentive and ready to serve.

6 – There are Spiritist Centers that reserve certain rooms exclusively for mediumistic meetings; in so doing they try to preserve the mediumistic environment. Is this reasonable?
► These rooms would be vacant for most of the 168 hours available per week. In other words, restricting the occupation of a room to one meeting only during a seven day time period would result in a very low percentage of use. Even if the rooms were used for mediumistic work everyday there would still be a lot of time left. There's no problem with using them for other activities such as Spiritist youth groups, children's education, courses, etc.

7 – Doesn't being so liberal with the use of these rooms risk contamination with energies that are not compatible with a mediumistic meeting and, therefore, undermine their effectiveness?
► The spirit mentors eliminate this potentiality by performing a cleansing of the environment. We should be concerned with the team's psychic condition only. This is what determines the meeting's usefulness.

8 – Does soft music contribute to a better meeting?
► Maybe, but there are two considerations. First there is the conditioning which may result when mediums become overly dependent on the music. Second is that not everyone likes a musical background. Some may experience difficulty in concentrating.

Difficulties

1 – There are mediums who need a magnetic pass after the meeting to come back to normal. Is this reasonable?
▶ It's natural for a medium to feel residual impressions from suffering entities who manifest through them; however, they disappear in a few minutes. If we get used to giving passes we create a conditioning situation.

2 – There are mediums who wait for the director to stand by them in order to transmit a manifestation. Is it an advisable practice?
▶ It's another conditioning. It may happen that the director comes close because of a hearing problem or because the medium is speaking too low. We can resolve these difficulties by asking the medium to avoid whispering, which many do during the channeling.

3 – We often notice that the counselor lowers his or her voice, speaking in a softer tone, when talking to spirits. Is there any inconvenience in doing this?
▶ Everything that is not natural is inconvenient. We should talk to the 'dead' as we do with the 'living'. The medium, as well as the counselor, must be aware that the entire group should be able to hear what they're saying so that they can pay attention, which is fundamental to the successful outcome of the work.

4 – What about manifestations from very young children in a mediumistic meeting?
▶ Common sense tells us that discarnate children do not wander about in an unconscious state, in need of explanations. Their lives aren't compromised by addictions and worldly passions. They experience no difficulty in being rescued by family members or institutions from the spirit world after they

have passed on.

5 – Is it an animistic process then, something from the medium's mind, when children manifest?
▶ It could be. In most cases, however, we are dealing with someone who regressed to a childish behavior. They're mental patients who escaped their problems by behaving like children. It's what happens to these spirits. Also, we should not dismiss the possibility that we're dealing with mocking spirits.

6 – Why do mediums find difficulty in transmitting names, dates and details about the life of the manifesting spirit?
▶ It's necessary to reiterate, always, that mediums are not telephones. They capture the spirit's mental flow of ideas, their impressions, sensations and ideas - but without details. Therein lies the difficulty.

7 – Should we avoid asking these types of questions?
▶ It depends on the communication. Sometimes the spirit insists on transmitting a particular message or something similar. In a case like this we should try, especially because some mediums are able to handle details.

8 – Why is it that in some meetings manifestations are delayed? What should we do?
▶ This usually happens with new teams because of mediums' inexperience; they hesitate, are afraid of exposing themselves, and this inhibits the interaction. We should wait a few minutes and sustain the energy, steady thoughts, empathy, and good will to support our companions who were drafted for mediumistic labor. If nothing happens, we end the meeting for the day.

Guides

1 – Do all mediumistic meetings have spirit directors?
▶ Yes, provided that the organization is under a Spiritist orientation respectful of the edifying purposes and learning opportunities which should characterize them.

2 – So will there not be mentors if there is not special care? If we hold a meeting for mere curiosity or immediate interests?
▶ Spirits may manifest, but they won't be evolved spirits who are capable of directing the meeting efficiently. Mentors with such capability have more important matters to take care of.

3 – The determining factor then is the group's motivation?
▶ Exactly. This affects not only the type of mentors, but also the spirits who will be counseled. When I was an adolescent, I participated in a group that was determined to unmask mystifying spirits for the sport of it, not for enlightened purposes. Not one mentor from elevated strata ever came to our meeting. And if a mentor tried to warn the group, it would risk to be taken for a mystifying spirit.

4 – Can it happen that a team is guided by obsessing spirits?
▶ Yes, if the team is organized for immediate interests. There are mediums who only work for a price and commercialize their talents; they're usually tormented or assisted by substandard spirits. They usually transmit orientations that supposedly come from spirit mentors but are in fact, from obsessors who assail the person asking for help.

5 – What conclusion can you draw about mediumistic groups in which all the mediums receive their own guides?
▶ It's indicative of animism; guides have more important tasks to do; they wouldn't limit themselves to merely saying hello and then stand idly by their 'instruments."

6 – *Isn't it desirable to hear the mentors when the groups are guided by spirit mentors?*

▶ No doubt, provided there are mediums capable of conveying the manifestation; but the development of this ability requires experience, study, and discipline over a long period of time. New groups shouldn't worry about this. They should let it happen naturally.

7 – *There are groups in which mediums let their guides manifest at the end of the meeting for a 'psychic cleansing'. Is this a good practice?*

▶ What if the guide doesn't manifest? Would the medium stay unclean? It's another type of conditioning that must be avoided. Mediums should be feeling well after a meeting, conscious of duties accomplished, healthy and in peace.

8 – *How can we be sure that the manifesting spirit, who says he's a mentor, is speaking the truth?*

▶ We have to apply Kardec's wisdom here. We must analyze the content; observe the language, the form, and the intention. We must remember the elemental principle that superior spirits only engage themselves in enlightening work with clear objectives and such spirits use words that clarify and amplify our understanding.

The Great Example

1 – *Where do you place Chico Xavier in the Spiritist context?*

▶ A definitive appreciation of a historical persona requires time. However we can attest to what is common sense: Chico Xavier is someone who parted waters. Spiritism in Brazil is divided into "before" and "after" him, that's how significant and impressive was his contribution.

2 – What would you emphasize in Chico Xavier, the man?
▶ It is commonly said that geniuses must be appreciated from a distance because co-existing with them is problematic. Chico was an exception. It's difficult for people who were fortunate enough to share his company to pick an area where he was greatest, whether it was his contribution to Spiritism or his example of humility and dedication to the Good that gained the respect and admiration even of those who combat Spiritism.

3 – Chico was of humble origin, poor family, physical problems, limited eyesight... Was he paying off karmic debts in spite of his elevated mission?
▶ I don't see his problems as trials involving compensation for past debts but as a personal choice. Evolved spirits frequently ask for pain and difficulty when they come to earth so that they may not be careless. If everything is easy, even missionaries can be distracted away from their commitments.

4 – Besides the iron grip of pain, and inclination for solidarity, to what else would you attribute his success?
▶ The discipline that marked his work; he followed the guidance of his spiritual mentor, Emmanuel, faithfully. This was the virtue that Emmanuel stressed when Chico asked him what was the basic requirement to achieve his mediumistic mandate.

5 – What would you highlight from the books that Chico channeled?
▶ The romances, Emmanuel's evangelical commentaries, poetry, particularly "Parnasus de Além Tumulo"[13], the

---

13   Translator's Note: "Anthology from Beyond the Grave", not yet translated into English.

admirable chronicles by Humberto de Campos, thousands of messages from spirits who wanted to console grieving relatives and, above all, the monumental Andre Luiz collection.

6 – There are people who contend that texts received from Andre Luiz are mere fantasy, particularly because they're from an indebted spirit who spent eight years in the lower zones.
▶ I think it's idle chat, especially because Andre Luiz was a member of a team that Emmanuel organized and supervised. What we need to emphasize is that his texts conform to the Spiritist codification. His books extend the knowledge base by providing an amplified spiritual vision and the relationship between earth and the beyond.

7 – Who will be Chico's successor?
▶ Gabriel Delanne, Leon Denis, and Camille Flammarion were Kardec's collaborators, not his successors. Something similar occurs with Chico. All of us writers and mediums who are dedicated to the dissemination of Spiritism, act as *distributors* for this wonderful *wholesaler* of Spiritist works; his inestimable contribution complements and expands Kardec's codification.

8 – Will Emmanuel and Andre Luiz, who oversaw Chico's mission, be able to continue their wonderful work by using other mediums?
▶ Only they could say it. Anyway, I believe that if they do, they won't identify themselves. They'll prefer anonymity to avoid sterile conflicts as to the authenticity of their manifestations. They know better than we do that it's the content of the message that is important, not the signature.

Made in the USA
Lexington, KY
13 November 2010